T0196910

Grace
UPON
GRACE

Christ The Everlasting Fountain of Life

TERESIA W. MUTISO, PHD

WESTBOW
PRESS
A DIVISION OF THOMAS NELSON
& ZONDERVAN

Scripture taken from the New American Version of the Bible.

This is a work of fiction. All of the characters, names, incidents, organizations, and dialogue in this novel are either the products of the author's imagination or are used fictitiously.

WestBow Press books may be ordered through booksellers or by contacting:

WestBow Press
A Division of Thomas Nelson & Zondervan
1663 Liberty Drive
Bloomington, IN 47403
www.westbowpress.com
1 (866) 928-1240

Because of the dynamic nature of the Internet, any web addresses or links contained in this book may have changed since publication and may no longer be valid. The views expressed in this work are solely those of the author and do not necessarily reflect the views of the publisher, and the publisher hereby disclaims any responsibility for them.

Any people depicted in stock imagery provided by Thinkstock are models, and such images are being used for illustrative purposes only.
Certain stock imagery © Thinkstock.

ISBN: 978-1-5127-3419-5 (sc)
ISBN: 978-1-5127-3418-8 (e)

Library of Congress Control Number: 2016904055

Print information available on the last page.

WestBow Press rev. date: 04/07/2016

Contents

Dedication

To all the many wonderful people who have helped me in my quest for knowledge, in my journey of spiritual life, and for all those who will have the opportunity to read the thoughts shared here.

Preface

One summer day during a quiet time in a retreat, I observed water jets welling up from within a fountain and gushing continuous streams of water. Sun rays from above seemed to kiss the water streams, as the water jets buoyed and danced to the wind. The water jets flowed continuously and effortlessly. In a moment I was transfixed to a deeper reality, that Christ is described as the everlasting fountain of life. The water represented grace, freely given, freely flowing to all who dare to believe and trust in God's promises. There was born in me, a strong desire to put this in writing and this consequently led to the writing of these pages.

Additionally, during this year of mercy, the personal witness and teaching of Pope Francis on joy of the Gospel and the mercy of God, has been like the miracle of the wine in the wedding at Cana. It's fresh and reinvigorating, raising the dreams and hopes of many Christians and people of good will, all over the world. This has profoundly influenced my reflections and writing of this work.

Introduction

We live in a world where there is explosion of noise and so many options to choose from. The Television alone has about 189 cable TV channels. Unsuspecting consumers are bombarded with so many ads; it is almost impossible to make a sound decision. There seems to be continuous news of world catastrophe, a child molested. Refugees fleeing from war. Broken families. Then talk about the throw away culture; fast food, fast marriage and everything else seems disposable. All these can bring a weariness of spirit and confusion, unless we find something profound to direct our choices, focus our attention and fill our lives with.

This book is an attempt to offer a sense of direction and share some practical ways to center our lives, during this jubilee year of mercy. At a deeper level, it's a prayer sharing, from a seekers heart to another. It is easy to identify with the Michelangelo's non-finito statue[1] of the trapped prisoner. According to Michelangelo, the sculptor is a tool God uses simply to reveal the already magnificent figures existing in the marble. The sculptor task is to cut away the excess, to reveal. It's further hypothesized that non-finito represents the eternal struggle of humans being to free themselves from material trappings. This endless struggle of man to free himself from his physical control is a symbol of the flesh burdening the soul. The prisoner seems to be calling to the artist (God) to set him free. This is so true in our lives, we spent most of time our reading self-help books, motivational, inspirational and better yourself books, because we have somehow figured out that the challenge of being the perfect self we were meant to be, has nothing to do with the external circumstances we find ourselves in. It is the internal struggles which are tough to overcome. If we follow Michelangelo's thought, we have all our perfection within us already; we just need to chip away all the imperfections we have accumulated to reveal the finest self from within.

God has said that he created the human person in his own image and likeness. He is the king; we are the princesses and princess of the almighty God. But for most part of our lives we spent our time running around in dirt like the chickens, while we were meant to be flying high and gliding the skies like the eagles.

Again we are like drums and God is the drummer. It would be interesting if drums started resisting and protesting about the rhythms to be produced. A drum responds to the drummer. Or, we can be likened to a pen used in calligraphy; the penmanship will produce a beautiful writing using a pen or brush. We are like the marble, the brush and the drum, if we let God be the artist; He will reveal our authentic self.

May God continue to surround you with his light and love as you go through these pages.

Fountain of life

What is a fountain? Wikipedia, the free encyclopedia[2] describes a fountain as a Latin word for "fons" (a source, or a spring) which is a pierce of architecture which pours out water into a basin or jets it into the air. Fountains in middle ages were associated with source of life, wisdom, innocence. If we browse the internet there are countless representations of fountains from all over the world and particularly in most of the major cities.

Additionally, we find a rich description of fountain in the Bible. Palestine is a country of undulating mountains and hills and it is abundant in fountains of water. These fountains are termed as the bright sparkling "eyes" of the desert and are said to be remarkable for their abundance and their beauty, especially on the west of the Jordan area[3]. All the perennial rivers and streams of the country are supplied from the fountains, and depend comparatively little on the surface water. The murmur of the water is heard in every small valley and the luxuriant foliage which surrounds them is seen in every plain (Deut; 8:7, 11:11). The reservoirs acted as the heart of the surrounding village. Most of these fountains were natural. Naturally, the women exchanged news as they drew water and the young men met, exchanged news as they watered their family herd of cattle.

In our present day cities, most of the fountains are man-made with drinking fountain, providing clean drinking water in the public building, the parks, and in the public places. Spray pool allows city residents to wet and cool off in the summer.

Figurative use of Fountain in the Bible.
God; the source of living waters.

In a number of instances in the Bible, God is considered as the fountain of life. Therefore, if God is the fountain of life, we can draw life from him continuously. The psalmist, in psalm 36:9, expresses God's providence when he goes on to say that, we feast on the rich food of God's house, who gives us to drink from his delightful stream. For God is the fountain of life. If we depend on God for sustenance, we are sure to live. He will provide for our needs, both the physical and spiritual. We find this echoed again in the writings of prophet Jeremiah, when he touts the children of Israel, against their infidelity to God. Prophet Jeremiah laments that the children of Israel have forsaken God, the source of living waters and then, instead dug for themselves cisterns which are broken holding no water. Again the prophet reiterates that the rebels in the land of Israel shall be put to shame because they have abandoned their God; the source of living waters (Jeremiah2:13; 17:13). The children of Israel allowed other Gods to replace their God. They started to worship the neighboring Gods. They intermingled and intermarried adopting new polytheist lifestyle. This can be so true to us too, we can adopt worldly life style allowing it to influence our choices and decisions. For example, we may rationalize that it's okay to be worldly because, everybody is. The truth is what is popular may not always be right and what is right may not always be popular. Let's be vigilant to avoid imitating popular culture if it does not augur well with our Christian values.

Divine pardon and purification, with an obvious Messianic reference

In the final chapters of Prophet Zachariah, he describes the final assault of the enemy on Jerusalem, after which the messianic age of Christ begins. "On that day there shall be open to the house of David and to the inhabitants of Jerusalem, a fountain to purify from sin and uncleanness. (Zechariah 13:1) This is contrasted to the writing in the book of numbers, which describes the lustral water used for purification rites for those who were unclean. The Israelites prepared the lustral water with ashes from a burnt red heifer. (Numbers 19: 9, 13, 20; 31: 23). This purification of the children of Israel using the lustral waters made of ashes of the burnt heifer foreshadowed Christ, the high priest who offered his life to purify the human race of sin and make us acceptable to the father.

> "for if the blood of goats and bulls and the sprinkling of a heifer's ashes can sanctify those who are defiled, so that their flesh is cleansed, how much more will the blood of Christ, who through the eternal spirit offered himself unblemished to God, cleanse our consciences from dead works to worship the living God", (Hebrews 9: 11-14)

This is the good news that the son of God come down to assume our human form and to finally die for our redemption. Jesus has paid for our past, present and future sins. This is captured again in the first letter of Peter 1:18 " realizing that you were ransomed from your futile conduct, handed on by your ancestors, not with perishable things like silver or gold, but with the precious blood of Christ as of a spotless unblemished lamb". If this does not capture our attention, then we are in a sad state, because probably we have become indifferent, or numb to this reality of God's immerse love for us. Can you imagine how we would react if we were sentenced to death and then our own biological father decided that he would take our place and not only that, but also atone for any other crime we would ever commit. It would awaken a transforming decision in our own lives. Possibly, we would never forget that. But for some reason we take Jesus dying on the cross for us lightly, like it happened way back then, and therefore, we are far removed from the experience.

This idea of messianic purification is further noted in the book of Revelation 1: 5 which refer to Christ as one who has freed us or washed us of our sins with his flowing blood, "to him who loves us and has freed us from our sins by his blood". In the book of First John 1: 7, the epistle also links the purification of our sins with the blood of Jesus, with striving to live in the light and being reconciled to one another; "but if we walk in the light as he is in the light, then we have fellowship with one another, and the blood of his son Jesus cleanses us from all our sins" it's vital to note that this redemption in Christ is freely given by God to us because Jesus atoned for our sins by his blood. During the last supper, Jesus was to seal the new covenant by shedding of his blood.

In addition, this concept of Divine pardon and purification can be further associated with the sacrament of penance which is announcing freedom from sin through the death and the resurrection of Jesus Christ. The Catholic encyclopedia[4] points out that in the early church, the sacrament of penance was referred to as the second baptism. It explains that this baptism is brought about through tears of the penitent. Actually the church is said to possess both the water and the tears; the waters of baptism and the tears of penance. Though the church is Holy, its members need purification and renewal. In the sacrament of penance the faithful obtain mercy from God, pardon for their sins and are reconciled with the church. Thus, Jesus is the living fountain who saves human kind from the clutches of sin by means of his sacrifice in Calvary, blood and water flows freely setting all free if we dare accept his grace. Pope Francis encourages us to constantly contemplate the mystery of mercy. It is the fountain of joy, serenity and peace. Pope Francis continues to affirm that God's mercy will always be greater than any sin we commit and that no-one can place limits on the love of God. God is ever ready to forgive. (Pope Francis, 2015)[5]

Wisdom and godliness

To offer just a little background on the book of proverbs, the book was written to teach wisdom and fear of the lord. First of all, the book was directed towards the young and the inexperienced. Secondary, it was also to assist those who desired to advance in gaining and training in wisdom. The young and inexperienced may have a twofold meaning. First it refers to young people as relates to age. But this may also be referring to young in knowledge of the lord, irrespective of years. And this young in faith or knowledge can be a real challenge to identify because not all people take the time to grow in knowledge and reflection of the bible in their lives. The teaching of the wise is like a fountain of life that a man may use to avoid the snares of death. How does man avoid snares of death? One wonders. Sin clearly leads to death and thus sin can be termed as death. For example let's imagine the sin of coveting others wealth or fame. We may start with just pre-occupation, like how we could be happy with some of their wealth. Then with more pre-occupation, we may be tempted to steal. This brings in the sin of corruption, or stealing, with negative effects to the person and to the society. The person may kill, or be killed in the process of stealing. If not, they may be jailed leaving their family to suffer.

According to the book of Prophet Malachi 3:20, it is written that those who fear the lord, there will arise, the sun of justice with its healing rays. The teaching of the wise was to act as a compass or a geographical positioning system (GPS) devise which makes it easier to navigate long journeys, sometimes to unknown destinations. These devices tell you which routes options are reliable, have less traffic, or where to exit if you need to refresh. The same way, the teaching of the wise was to direct people making their journey of life toward their promised land (Heaven). It would show one how to get there faster and the obstacles to avoid along the way. For we are all sojourners and pilgrims to our heavenly home.

Damascene[7] in his book "The fountain of knowledge or wisdom" writes that nothing is more estimable than knowledge, for he suggests that knowledge is the light of the rational soul. Damascene encourages all to approach that teacher in whom there is no falsehood, and who is the truth. He continues to show that Christ is the subsistent wisdom and truth; in Christ are all the hidden treasures of knowledge, who gives wisdom and power of God the father. He argues us, to learn from true knowledge of all the things that are. This is in line with the teaching and reflections of Pope Francis who urges us to find and set a consistent time to read, and meditate on the word of God and slowly he will reveal his gaze to us (Pope Francis, 2015). It is interesting to note that the Bible or the word of God is more than alive, bringing new awareness every day if we dare to ponder on it a new. It is totally possible that if we read and applied the passages of the Bible every day, the passages would speak to us a new every time. Most likely we would have a new depth of understanding each time we read and reflect on it.

Children

Deuteronomy is the last book of Pentateuch which was written after Israelites had been occupants of the Promised Land for a long time. The simile of a fountain is used to represent Israelites offspring's. "Israel had dwelt securely, and the fountain of Jacob had been undisturbed, in a land of grain and wine, where the heavens drip with dew. (Deuteronomy 33:28)

There is almost a sense of filial pride when talking about the fountain of Israel being undisturbed. One senses the beauty, the majestic and fecundity of the descendants of Israel in the serene surroundings. This is a rich symbol to think of children as a fountain of life. Another similar symbol is to see children, like a cluster of ripe grapes. It symbolizes a sense of blessings and bounty. One can almost hear the laughter, the music and the joyous dancing of youths, like a clear fountain on a sunny day spraying out soothing and beautiful hues of jets of water to the surrounding.

In what ways can we make Children like the fountain of life?

It is common knowledge and practice in all cultures to protect water sources, because 'water is life'. The same can be said to all of the children of the world, they need to be protected and nurtured so that they can grow secure and undisturbed, secure both physically and emotionally. The first place children need to feel secure is in their homes. A child truly loved by the parents grows to be a secure person. No money or material things can replace the power of unconditional love and presence of a parent. As a child or young person negotiate through the developmental changes and the growing pains of life, it's the parental presence which will assist and shield a child from life's challenges like the cyber bullies and the predators. Let's protect our children for they are the source of life for the future generations. There are different ways, and activities which can help parents bond with their children, like baking together on Sundays or holidays, fishing, family camping out, singing corals as a family, praying and eating together. Other ritual which can be helpful is blessing of children before going to sleep, going to school or when children are going away from home. Parents can formulate their own simple and meaningful blessings, or they can adopt formal ones like the Aarons blessings; "The lord bless and keep you, may he make his face to shine upon you and be gracious to you, may he act kindly towards you and give you peace" (Numbers 6:24-26). These rituals though simple become a foundation for children's relationship with the Heavenly father. If we believe a picture is worth a thousand words, how much more a lived experience about an earthly father representing a God who we do not see but who we must love and trust. Children can only give what they have, what they have is mostly what they have been given throughout their lives. If they were given love, they will in turn feel loved and give out love, if valued, they will value others and if blessed, they will become a blessing unto others. Hence forth parents should not underestimate their influence on their children and indirectly on the world. It may be easier to curse the world for its ills, but if each parent tried and put their best efforts in raising their children, reflecting what they would like the world to look like, this would be likened to lighting one candle instead of cursing the darkness, and soon, there will be enough light to illuminate the whole world, building the legacy we all long to experience and see.

Prosperity

It's almost a natural phenomenon where there is a spring of water there is abundant growth of trees and foliage. Imagine that time in ancient past, during the period our ancestors were hunters and gathers, they would go to the springs of water to quench their thirst, as well as hunt for the many animals also looking for drinking water themselves. The surrounding areas would also provide berries and eatable roots for their nourishment. Water source was associated with sustenance of life.

Then during the early settlement communities were founded around a spring of water for the same purposes. The fountains became the life and center of the village. Woman met there to collect water. The spring provided water for the livestock and its water was used for irrigation. The springs of water were not only beautiful but also sustained all life.

In Psalms, the psalmist uses the symbol of springs of water to indicate prosperity. God is declared to have changed the desert into pools of water and, dry land into a spring of water which helped them reap abundant harvest. (Psalms 107:35). The psalmist understood God's all-powerful ability to bless them and turn barren land into orchard of blessings. This is still applicable to us, God's children today. God can turn our barren circumstances into oasis of blessings. God's miracles were not only meant for the Old Testament people. Sometimes it's easy to dismiss God's greatness because we are afraid to hope for more than our share of good things. But the reality is that we cannot exhaust Gods blessings. There is more than enough for each and every one of his children. God gives us only according to our ability to receive. So why do we limit ourselves to the barest minimum when God is promising us all the blessings materially and spiritually? Let's pause for a while and imagine that God had provided containers of different volumes, ranging from a few milliliters to a million liters and our job was just to pick whatever we wanted for God to fill it with blessings and let's assume that was true for everything else precious in life. We would all agree it would be absurd to choose the tiniest of the containers. Generally speaking, we would pick a large container enough for ourselves and may be a little to spare. This example is over simplified, but of course we need to work hard, be displine and do the best we can and then trust God to bring all things together to bear abundant fruits.

Again God is seen to have turned the rocks into pools of water and the stone into flowing springs.(Psalm114:8) this can be contrasted with prophet Hosea 13:15, on how the children of Israel will lose their wealth if they continued to sin. The prophet's lamented that an east wind will come from the lord, rising from the desert and will dry up the spring, and leave their fountain dry and destroy the land of every precious thing as a result of sin.

Although we cannot take this literally, that if we have less means or are sick or suffering its only because we have sinned against God. But, if we take sin to mean that we are out of relationship with others, our environment and God, then, this would make some sense. If we are not centered on God, then we are centered on ourselves or any other idol which creates some imbalance in our lives. For example, over indulging in alcohol could be disastrous, although alcohol is good in itself if taken in moderation; the chance we turn into alcoholics is very high. Then the other complications associated with it follow, like failed relationships, broken families, unemployment, poor health and probably death. Another example would be over indulging with the internet, one could become so addicted that everything else in life suffers. One has less time for exercise; to relax, and of course less time for people one cares about. Though internet surfing in itself is a harmless action, overdoing it can alienate us from ourselves, others and God. This alienation then becomes sin and can lead to death indirectly. Sin does not bring life, but rather diminishes life. Thus sin in many ways leads to misery and death.

In the book of prophet Ezekiel 47:1-12, the great and superabundant stream flowing from the temple restores fertility to the barren ground. " Along the river banks I saw very many trees on both sides..., where the river flows every sort of living creature that can multiply shall live, and there shall be abundant fish," water indicates great blessings while dryness signifies a curse. This wonderful stream symbolizes the return to the initial paradise, (Genesis: 10-14.) the Garden of Eden with its rivers. But in the real sense, this vision from the book of prophet Ezekiel could also really signify the spiritual aspect of the temple. The temple was seen as a source of blessing and grace flowing like a river and giving life wherever it passes. Likewise it was believed that those who worshipped in the temple would be filled with every kind of blessings. This takes us back to the Garden of Eden, where there were trees of every kind and God walked in harmony with Adam and Eve before the fall.

Likewise, if we want to live life filled with abundance of blessing, we need to worship God in spirit and truth, in our souls and recognize the same God in other souls, where God dwells. Then blessings and grace will overflow and bless others wherever we go. We will become a river of grace flowing out to others. Those we touch will flower and manifest all fruits of Holy Spirit. Our presence and witness will become a channel of grace for others. Grace will overflow from the temple "our souls" becoming a stream bringing life wherever it passes.

Jesus life was a true source of blessings for the whole of human kind. At the beginning of his public life Jesus read from the scroll where it is written. (Luke 4:18)

"The spirit of the lord is upon me, because he has anointed me to bring glad tidings to the poor. He has sent me to proclaim liberty to captives and recovery of sight to the blind, to let the oppressed go free, and to proclaim a year acceptable to the lord"

Jesus came to restore to wholeness the down trodden and lift them up them from their lowly state, so that they can share in his life as children of God. This is also echoed in the magnificant, the song of Mary after greeting her cousin Elizabeth, where she mentioned that her soul glories God because he had looked in her lowliness and from then on all generations will call her blessed.

The book of Prophet Joel: 3:18 issue a prophetic picture of the salvation of the elect. The prophet mentions that the mountains shall drip with new wine and the hills shall flow with milk and the channels of Judah shall flow with water; a fountain shall issue from the house of the lord to water the land. These points to the wine of new understanding, the beatitudes, where new wisdom flows from. Jesus is the new fountain. There is new wine of understanding about the nature of God and His grace at work. God is full of loving kindness, slow to anger, abounding in goodness. In the mountain Jesus teaches about the beatitudes; blessed are those who are meek, merciful and those who hunger and thirst for God. Jesus mentions that the gentle shall inherit the land. The hills shall flow with the milk of goodness, where the lost, down trodden and forsaken are the first to enter the kingdom of God.

Life everlasting

Another important theme associated with the fountain of life is life eternal. In the book of Revelation 7:17, in the triumph of the elect, the Lamb who is Jesus Christ will lead the elect to springs of life giving water, which is the water of life referring to God's grace flowing from Christ.

Where do we seek for our sense of identity? Is it in the celebrities? Is it in our credentials? Is it in material things? Or is it in the life of Jesus Christ? How does one become the "elect"? Would it not be vanities of vanities to chase after the celebrities or attain all the education we can and surround ourselves with all the latest material items we can, and then on our death bed find that all these do not satisfy our deepest need? Or rather the question would be, can we experience fame, be wealthy and yet espouse the gospel values which will enable us to be counted among the elect? If we can use our fame to draw others to holiness and our education to enlighten those in doubt and our wealth to assist our brothers and sisters in need, then most likely we will have accomplished Christ's work and become life givers.

Additionally, in Rev 21:6; Jesus says, "He is the Alpha and the Omega, and to the thirsty he will give life giving water" Jesus transcends time and space. He existed before his natural birth and he continues to exist even after his physical death. To the thirsty, he will give life giving water. Who are the thirsty? And what are they thirsting for? Those are the ones who are searching for more. They have a longing which this world cannot satisfy. They long, and desire God to fill the void in their hearts. Jesus is promising life eternal for those who hunger for his word. It is easy to cheat ourselves, and try to satisfy our inner emptiness with material things, artificial relationships or in recreations like taking alcohol and/ or drugs. And since no created object can ever fill that void completely, we risk going through life chasing after the next new gig, thinking it will do the trick, until we discover that only God can do the trick. He is the answer. Once we make him the center of our lives, our life will have coherence and meaning in spite of whatever circumstances we find ourselves, politically, socially and /or economically. With his life giving grace, all else make sense.

In Rev 22: 1, the author continues with the same theme of life giving water and in the vision he saw an angel showing him the life giving water sparkling like crystal flowing from the throne of God and of the Lamb. In verse17, it's recorded that the spirit and the bride (church) say come and let the one who thirsty come forward, and the one who wants it, receive the gift of life- giving water. This thirsting for God has been captured well in Psalm 42 in the old testament of the Bible.

"As the deer longs for streams of water so my soul is longing for you O God. My being thirsty for God, the living God. When can I go and see the face of God"

In this particular Psalm, the psalmist is thought to be in the northern extreme part of Israel, far away from the temple of Jerusalem. The psalmist longs for the Divine presence which the children of Israel experienced in the temple worship. There is progression of the idea of life giving water from the image of the temple, to the church, and finally to the person of Jesus Christ, as in the personification of life giving water from his pierced heart. This is further echoed in Psalm 84:3 "my soul yearns and pines for the courts of the Lord, my heart and flesh cry out for the living God." This prayer of a pilgrim to Jerusalem temple expresses the strong longing to enjoy the divine presence during one of the annual feast to the Holy temple in Jerusalem. The psalmist continues to say that as they pass through the bitter valley (Baca Valley, probably on the way to Jerusalem) they find springs of water provided by God. The psalmist does not stop there in showing the goodness of the Lord, Gods benevolence is shown in that he also provided water from the pools for those who lose their way. He is not only quenching their thirst, he is also the divine provider on the way to Jerusalem.

In psalm 143:6, in a prayer of distress, the psalmist remembers Gods wondrous works in the past as he stretches out his hands to God, thirsting for God like a parched land. This captures the essence of prayer; it's the ultimate longing of the human heart to the living God. When a deer yearns for water, when a parched earth longs for the rain, nothing can stop the great desire each has for the life giving water. In a profound way this surmises the deepest longing of a human heart to connect with the creator "the living fountain". No wonder St. Augustine[8] understood this later in his life after being a seeker for this essence of life for a long time, and after seeking for answers in the wrong places.

St. Augustine says

> "Our hearts are restless until they rest in you O God. Late have I loved you, O Beauty ever ancient and ever new! And, behold, you were within me, and I out of me, and there I searched for you. You called and cried out loud and shattered my deafness. You were radiant and resplendent, you put to flight my blindness. You were fragrant, and I drew in my breath and now pant after you. I tasted you, and I feel but hunger and thirst for you. You touched me, and I am set on fire to attain the peace which is yours"

St. Augustine summarizes what most of us don't know how to put into words. The Divine romance between God and the human soul. It's like our souls have an innate need to be intimate with its creator.

Another symbol of life giving water is well developed in the story of the Samaritan woman. When the woman asked Jesus how he a Jew, can ask for water from her, a Samaritan woman? He replied "If you knew the gift of God and who is saying to you give me a drink, you would have asked him instead and he would have given you the living water" Jesus went further to explain that whoever drinks the water he gives will never thirsty again. He added that the water he gives will become a spring welling up to eternal life. (John 4:4-39).

Just like the Samaritan woman, initially, many a time we do not recognize who it is, who is speaking or asking us for help. When we are not in the grace of the moment it's hard to encounter and recognize Jesus in the other. The other can be any one who is not like us, the poor, the rich, the stranger, from a different church, tribe, race and the list goes on and on. Rather than concentrating on what we think they lack, in faith we ought to go ahead and meet their needs, considering Jesus teaching that any time we helped one of those in need/little ones, we did it to Jesus. Then instead of being quick to quip or assume that the other does not have the necessary tools for the business or anything of importance to offer we will notice that we are encountering Jesus, who is willing to give us living waters welling up to eternity. No wonder, God is said to have a sense of humor, we encounter him sometimes in places or situations where we least expect to find him.

Our life does not end in the encounter with Jesus; this is only the beginning of the story. Once we encounter Jesus like the woman, we become aware of our state of life as it is.Jesus meets us where we are, in a non-judgmental way. Like the Samaritan woman, we may have to leave our water jars behind and go and witness him to our communities. What is your water jar which you have to leave behind in order to witness Jesus to your peers? It is only you who know what that jar is. There is almost a sense of urgency, once we understand who Jesus is and what he can do in the lives of our friends and in our own lives. Jesus is likened to the fountain of water and thus continually pours grace upon grace into our souls. His abundant life giving blessings pours into our souls continuously filling, and refreshing us. He is the source and the center of our lives. The only condition is to avail and open our hearts to encounter and receive him. Then, witness him to our communities so that they too can discover for themselves who Jesus is and believe not because of our testimony but because they too have seen and experienced him.

We notice that when the apostles came back from buying lunch; they could not help wondering, what on earth was their master doing with this woman of questionable behavior? Don't we sound like the apostles most of the time? We are busy judging people based on their past history; in complete oblivious to what is happening in the present moment. The woman become an effective disciple within a few hours, and brought her entire community to believe in Jesus in a day. She had received so much grace that she could not contain the fire of the Holy Spirit. In our daily encounter with different people, let's remember that some people respond to God's call spontaneously, others take a while, while others like Judas the apostle though very close to Jesus never seemed to get it.

In Isaiah 55:1, in the invitation for grace, God calls those who are thirsty to come to the water. He beseeches us to come to him heedfully, and to listen to him so that we may have life. He promises to renew with us an everlasting covenant, according to the benefits assured to King David. This promise is fulfilled in Jesus the new and eternal covenant. Jesus is the living spring issuing grace into eternity. There is a great hymn[9] "come to the water" which is based on this text. "O let all who thirst, seek, toil and all the poor, let them come to the water, and let all who have nothing, let them come to the Lord: without money and without price". Jesus has already paid the price. He is the living spring welling up to the end of the time. What a blessing! Jesus longs for us; he desires our love, so that he can fill us with more eternal life. This prompts us to join with the psalmist in Psalm 63, and echo the song of ardent longing for God.

> "O God you are my God, for you I long! My body yearns for you, for my soul thirst for you, like a parched land, life-less without water. I will bless you as long as I live; I will lift up my hands in calling on your

name. My soul will savor the rich banquet of praise; with joyous lips my mouth shall honor you"

Let us then hurry up and approach the throne of grace so that we can draw water joyfully from the wells of salvation (Isaiah 12:3) Is it not sad that we walk along the journey of life thirsting for something more out of life, but often times, seeking for this abundant life in things, places and relationships which do not satisfy. Jesus promises to his followers that he is the way, the truth and the life, and whoever follows him will have eternal life. Let us then put Christ in his right place "the center of our lives and activities" and everything else in our lives will fall in place. He is the unchanging friend; yesterday, today and tomorrow. There is no price too expensive for him to pay for us, so that we can have access to his amazing grace. In the Holy Gospel according to John 3:16, it is written that "for he so loved the world that he send his only begotten son so that we may have life" and then Johns gospel goes on to exclaim that from his fullness we have received grace in place of grace. For some reason this idea of the Son of God dying for us has not registered as a reality for us. If we understood, we would be the most grateful creatures on earth. We sort of go around like we don't matter to anybody and particularly to Jesus, who laid his life down for us, so that, we are free indeed of our debts from sin and corruption. Below is a story depicting the love dance between God and a soul, portraying different levels of intimacy between God and a chosen soul.

A wealthy and kindly couple had wanted an heir after being married for about ten years but was unable to have a child. The couple had inherited a big track of land, large herd of livestock, and a number of large businesses. They had a mansion for a home, with a nice swimming pool, and a big fountain that fed the swimming pool. Many a time the couple would sit facing the beautiful fountain listening to the bubbling and the spraying of the water jets and wonder why God had not been pleased to favor them with a child. On this particular day Mona the wife sat watching the setting sun rays striking the water jets from the fountain, producing a splendid rain bow, she made a quiet petition to God, "just give me a child, even if it's a lame one, for me to hold and cherish" Monas husband found her in this state of deep desperation. In order to bring her some comfort, he assured Mona that they could always adopt a child, and after all they had each other to love and cherish. Meanwhile some of the laborers returned from the fields and since night was fast approaching the subject was dropped for the needs of the moment.

A year after this discussion at the fountain, Mona and her husband filed for adoption, and their excitement about the possibility of adopting a baby started to build up. Whether it was the excitement about filing for the adoption, and the anticipation associated with it, or it was God's way of answering Mona's prayer, it was exciting to behold. Mona discovered that she was expectant soon after. Mona delivered a baby boy and he was the joy of the family and indeed the whole village because Mona and her Husband were benevolent neighbors and charitable to those in need. The child was named Emanuel and Emanuel grew in stature and intelligence. His parents dotted on him, and he was beloved by many people. Emanuel was not only handsome; he was also very amiable and full of life. It was only natural to love him; he had that magnetic personality which seemed to pull people to him wherever he went.

Emanuel's parents sent him to the best schools, where he excelled in academic work and in extra curriculum activities. He manifested great potential for leadership. During the holidays he would come home with many friends and his parents had very high hopes for him. Who knows? He could become the president or whatever else he so choses to be, he had it all. Emmanuel acquired great grades in school; eventually he finished school and had a nice job. In time, he introduced a girl he had met in school to his parents who were beside themselves with happiness. God had been so gracious to them. Their only son felt like having more than a thousand children.

After a while Emanuel and his Girlfriend had an engagement party and as one would expect, it was an event which was talked about in the neighborhood for weeks. Their childhood friends, schoolmates and work mates were part of the celebration. It truly felt like a fairy tale. They planned to wed soon after and the wedding date was fast approaching, and all were in fever excitement in anticipation for this epic wedding of their beloved son and friend. Invitations were sent and arrangements were done in preparation for the big wedding day.

On the eve of by the wedding day, as the sun was setting, Emanuel's mother was caught up, by beauty of the fountain. The setting sun rays embraced the fountain water jets producing a myriad of spectacular rainbows. At that instant, she remembered that evening long time ago, when she prayed for a child even if it was a disabled one. She chuckled and shook her head in disbelief about how life had favored them since then. She said a blessing, praising God for his faithfulness. She brought herself back to the moment and continued with the lively preparation for the following day. Her heart was filled with gratitude.

The long anticipated day arrived, the sun was shining brightly, all parties had risen early and were dressed immaculately, truly, if there was a fairy tale wedding, it was going to be this one. The limousines ferried couples, brides maids, groomsmen and flower girls to the church. The church looked immaculate, the music was buoying, and smiling faces filled the air, it was simply ecstatic. This was going to be a wedding befitting a prince and a princess.

They were about to start the opening song, when Mona noticed some commotion outside the church. The commotion continued and people were coming towards her and her husband. One of their servants called them aside, informing them that there was a terrible accident just before the limousine carrying their son was about to exit from the main road to the church and it looked like there were no survivors. Mona just collapsed before hearing what actually happened to her son. Mona's husband felt like the ground was opening up under him and swallowing him towards the abyss, his son possibly dead, and his wife collapsing on hearing the news. What was one supposed to do?

Luckily the master of ceremony was near, and got the gist of the matter. He called for an ambulance to take Mona to the hospital. Then, the master of ceremony, Mona's husband and other relatives rushed to the accident scene. It did not look good. All the other three passengers and the driver had died on the scene. Emanuel was the only one spared but was critically injured. He was air lifted to the nearest trauma hospital. The master of ceremony and Mona's husband rushed to the fiancée and her parents to break the news. The fiancée collapsed upon hearing the news. Like Mona, her mother in law to be, she was rushed to the hospital. The joyous occasion had a three sixty turn round. The joyous morning, became a mourning session. No one had a dry eye. This was a nightmare, how does a day so unbelievably beautiful change so suddenly? The whole ceremony came to a standstill, the sadness was palpable; it just did not make sense. After about what felt like forever, though in reality it was just 15 minutes, the priest who was supposed to preside over the wedding called for calm, as he invited those who were willing, to have a service for comfort and God's healing grace. Some knelt, others sat unable to stand, and prayers started pouring out towards heaven, for Gods guidance and healing love.

In due course, information about Emmanuel started to fill in. The limousine had been hit by a truck with a drug driver who lost control and hit them head on. Emanuel sustained broken limbs, concussions and intensive internal injuries. The doctors who were taking care of Emanuel cautioned the father that even if Emmanuel survived, he may never regain fully his physical and mental functional capacities. It was a heavy blow to the parents, fiancée and the entire community. Weeks turned into months and Emanuel was still in coma. After seven months of intensive care and focused support from his fiancée and family, Emanuel started to show slight improvement. He started to react to pain. This was all the family needed to see to intensify their support. Meanwhile prayer vigils were held every week from different parts of the country for Emanuel's recovery. Emanuel's journey to recovery was long and odious; many times he wanted to give up. If it was not for the faith and the undying support from his family, fiancée and friends he would have given up. After two years he made an almost complete recovery, which to his doctors and many people, was miraculous.

His fiancée, family and friends were overjoyed and looked forward to him picking up and putting the pieces of his life back together. They looked forward to him rejoining the workforce, the party life which he was the center of, and then of course, marry his long awaited and faithful fiancée.

Emmanuel in time resumed working. But his fiancée noticed that something was quite different. Emmanuel was no longer the same. She confided this to Mona. Mona was convinced that this may be the after effects of his long hospital stay and re-assured her future daughter in law that all will be well. On his part Emanuel was quite listless, he knew something had changed in him and he could not quite put a finger onto it. He knew he needed more solitude and that he felt a void and a deep hunger within, which nothing seemed to satisfy. He was bewildered, he loved his fiancée and she had been there for him through thick and thin. Despite his deep appreciation something did feel very different and it was killing him inside.

He immersed himself in work to exorcise himself of whatever was accosting his life and making him restless. He simply became a workaholic to fill this void. Instead of marrying his fiancée, it looked like he was marrying his work. He finally confided to one of his dear friends, that he felt even emptier after attending the parties he used to be the king of. His friend suggested that he should see his primary care doctor because it may have something to do with his accident. He talked with his doctor, who like his mother thought that, it was the effects of the long illness and hospitalization.

One year after resuming his work, he was so aghast with God, how could God bring him out of the brink of the grave just to kill him in installment, it would be better if he had died like his friends,so he thought.

What was the use, he lamented. One evening after work, his emptiness became so unbearable that he decided to take a long drive. He came upon a church standing alone. He was drawn into it. The church was dark and quiet inside. On entering he started sobbing uncontrollably. He could not remember how long he stayed there and sobbed. Interestingly afterwards for whatever reason, he felt a great peace in his heart. It just felt so good. He was not crazy about going to eerie empty churches alone, but the peace he obtained from that church kept him coming back each evening. Each time he went, he promised himself that it would be the last; until he noticed he had become addicted. He looked forward to the time he spent alone in that church sometimes praying, other times just gazing at the tabernacle. He looked and felt happy again. It was ridiculous. His fiancée and friends started to suspect that he was seeing someone else privately.

Accidently in one of those evening visits, he met with a priest who was also praying in the church and started a conversation. He explained to the priest this 'strange behavior' of finding peace and solace in an empty church. The priest casually asked him if he had ever considered a priestly vocation. Emmanuel then told the priest about his near wedding to his fiancée and the rest of the sad events. The priest remembered that story because it had hit the headlines. The priest in a calm voice assured Emanuel that he would pray to the Holy spirit, and the spirit would make it clear to Emanuel somehow what he needs to do. He encouraged him to continue praying because if it was working for him, why change it?

After a long internal struggle, prayers and tears, Emanuel decided he was going to become a monk. His fiancé felt betrayed, his parents felt cheated, and his friends were troubled. Emanuel had God only for consolation, no one understood him. Why is he throwing his life away? To cut the long story short, though afraid, and unsure if he will manage it, Emmanuel finally entered a monastic life.

It did not take long for Emmanuel to start thriving in the monastery. He was a gifted singer, dedicated in his work and prayers, a charismatic leader and a sincere friend to those he came into contact with. What else would you look for in life? Life fell in place again and as nature would have it, he became the center of life even in the monastery. It was always a joy to be around Emanuel. In time Emanuel became a leader in the monastery, he immersed himself into prayer, worked and dedicated his time to run the affairs of the monastery.

Whoever said God must have a sense of humor must have had some interesting intimate experience with God. God was not finished with Emanuel. Emanuel had been relatively healthy since his major stay in the hospital. In the monastery he started to experience again, the inner sense of emptiness. He thought to himself, *"surely I have given God all, including the detachment from what was very dear to me, what possibly God could want from me"* he thought to himself. He was almost impatient with God.

This deep longing and emptiness became so intense that it was obvious to the other monks that something was going on in the life of Monk Emanuel. He met with his spiritual father who urged him to reduce his work and spend more time in prayer. Emmanuel did as he was advised but the void seemed to grow into a chasm. It was almost unbearable.

Emmanuel sought the help of a doctor who advised him that he could be suffering from depression or melancholy since he had not reconciled himself with his parents. He organized and met with his parents to see if he could feel better. The parents were still in pain, they had lost what was most dear to them, or so they thought. This had taken a great toll on their lives but they had clearly forgiven him.

Still he continued to experience a great emptiness until he decided to try even a deeper life of prayer in the dessert. After much prayer and discernment he set off for the dessert.

The journey was long and dangerous. He somehow got lost and spent more time on the journey than anticipated. His water and food supply were exhausted, and he relied on occasional tubers from shrubs for water and food. His physical hunger and thirst started to match his spiritual hunger and thirst. He was one man thirsting for more than life itself. Despite all this he trusted that the God of Providence, who had spared him from death, would surely protect him all over again.

This was another test of his faith, the sun was brazing hot, and the desert sand was steaming hot. He could not lie down, nor sit; the inactivity would kill him even faster. He had lost all sense of direction and time. He longed for the night, so that he could lie down, and die if this was what God intended for him; to die alone in a dessert thirsting for water, food and God. Evening came and Emanuel lay down thanking God for his life, and commending his soul into God's hands. Emmanuel was awakened by strange noises during the night; he was too weak to run away. He waited for his fate to unfold, and behold a Caravan of traders with camels came upon him. They took pity on him, and gave him water and food. They asked him where he hailed from and what business had brought him to a lonely dessert? He explained his mission and how his food supply had diminished. He learned that he was not far from a beautiful oasis of water. The caravan offered to take him to the spot since they were headed in that direction.

Emanuel was overjoyed that the lord had still been faithful to him; he did not leave him to die. His rescuers travelled with him to a place surrounded by foliage, and filled with cricket songs. They took him to a sheltered spot, where the overhead rock formed a natural roof. Since they had to continue after replenishing their camels, and refiling their water containers, they left Emanuel with some food supply and items they deemed he might need. Before leaving they asked for Emanuel's blessing, and he gladly blessed them. Emmanuel was soon overtaken by great sleep due to the journeys fatigue and heat. He fell into a deep slumber. He was awakened by bright a light which blinded his eyes, and filled his natural lodging. A white rabbit and her young ones were snuffling his hair. This was the best sleep he could remember of his life. He stretched himself remembering the events of the last few days and how he had ended up st that place. He had not felt this good in days. He strolled outside to survey his surroundings.

There were wild berries and thick foliage of green trees all around. It was a marvel to behold such presence of life in the dessert. He could hear the sound of birds. He followed the sound and found himself gazing at the most beautiful water fountain from the rocks which formed a green blue lagoon on the base. The birds were flying on top of the lagoon, occasionally winging in the sprays of the water fall. He was transfixed by the beauty, the waterjets from the waterfall formed myriads of rainbows. The rainbows seemed to be caught up in a dance of ethereal beauty. All of a sudden heaven and earth seemed to have embraced and Emanuel was caught in the beauty of it. In that moment his life struggles seemed to fade. The past, present and future became one explosion of a desire to be one with his Creator. He had this deep spiritual awareness that divine healing had transformed not only himself but his other relationships, his parents; his would have been bride, and his friends.

No words could explain this experience. He had become one with the fountain, with the rainbow, the birds, and all creation. There seemed to be a fountain, opened up from the heavens, passing through him and spreading unstoppably throughout the land.

It was the beginning of a new chapter of his life and he knew he would savor every minute of it. He knew what it meant to say "God alone suffices" Interestingly during the same time; his mother was going through a spiritual re- awakening. She sat watching her own fountain, in front of her house. She remembered how she had prayed for a child; even if the child would be disabled. She praised God for his faithfulness and asked for forgiveness for questioning Gods actions and wisdom in their life. Her blindness had been healed, instinctively she understood, in losing her son to God; she had gained more than the whole world. Mona and her husband felt truly blessed.

In the following months, Emanuel's former fiancée came to see the parents of Emanuel. She had married and had three children. She and her husband asked if they could purchase part of the property from Emanuel's family so that they could live next to them. Emmanuel's parents became like Godparents and grandparents to the children of Emmanuel's former fiancée. Mona and her husband lived to praise God. His blessing was like a fountain of grace flowing continuously, refreshing and renewing every life that it comes in contact with. God had worked mysteriously in their lives and they were all indeed blessed.

Grace upon Grace

There are many descriptions of grace in the online[9] dictionary; like simple elegance or refinement in movement. Other acronyms associated with grace are poise, gracefulness, finesse, suppleness, favor, pleasing appearance, charming, sense of propriety or thoughtfulness or a short prayer said at meals.

A second definition according to the Catholic Encyclopedia is that there are three common accepted references for the word Grace. In the first incident, it stands for something freely given and unmerited, as in divine assistance given to humans for regeneration or sanctification. A state of sanctification enjoyed through Divine favor. It's a spontaneous gift from God to man; the free and unmerited favor of God as manifested in the salvation of sinners and the bestowal of blessings. Divine grace then can be attributed as a freely given supernatural divine assistance to mankind. In different writings, in article 2, on grace and justification[10], grace is defined as favor, the free and underserved assistance that God gives mankind to respond to his call and become Gods children, adopted sons, sharing in his divine nature and of eternal life. The catechism of the Catholic Church further describes the grace of Christ as the gratuitous gift that God makes to us of his life, infused by the Holy Spirit into our souls to heal it of sin and to sanctify it.

Another description of Grace according to Pohle (1909)[11] is that Grace (*gratia, Charis*), in general, is a supernatural gift of God to intellectual creatures men and Angels for their eternal redemption, whether the latter be fostered and achieved through salutary acts or a state of holiness. Sanctifying grace (Habitual grace) refers to the conversion of Christians to the adopted children of God. To share in the divine life which God offers created persons is a real renewal, a second birth. Christians enjoy a new life which is their own. Additionally, grace refers to the very gift itself, as in the favor granted at court. Finally, grace can either be sanctifying/ habitual or actual grace. The sanctifying grace is habitual gift, a mystical disposition that perfects the soul to empower it to live with God and our actions to be persistently guided by his love. A good example would be in the life of Holy Mary Mother of Jesus. She was always in a state of grace. Habitual grace is distinguished from actual graces which refer to Gods intervention at initial conversion or during the process of one's sanctification.

The Roman Catholic Church teaching is clear that the seven sacraments are the means through which Christ through the Holy spirit confer grace to those disposed to receive grace. These are termed as the sacramental graces. Flynn[12] summarizes grace as participation in God's life, introducing us to the union of holy trinity. He further points out that Grace is Christ's own life poured into our souls to make us whole.

Then, there are the special graces termed as charisms (Greek word for favor) these graces which sometimes can be extra ordinary are aimed for the edification, and the common good of the church. For example if one has the gift of preaching, the preacher's homily will be filled with the Holy Spirit. People would be deeply moved. Sometimes, when one listens to the preaching, one is almost convinced that the preacher knows about his/her personal details or else somebody must have talked about him/her to the preacher. But in actual fact, it's the Holy Spirit at work. Another example would be anointed hymns, when you listen to the songs; it's like a healing balm to the soul. The sacred hymns express what humanly can't be put into words. After listening one feels a sense of happiness or one is challenged to take action and change a situation. To summarize, although grace is really a mystery, it can be studied as sanctifying, actual, habitual, sacramental efficacious and sufficient. Though there are seven sacraments used confer to grace; we will dwell slightly on the Eucharist and penance.

The Eucharist

The Eucharist particularly is seen as the source of grace since it represents the person of Jesus Christ. Thus the Eucharistic banquet is like an ocean of grace flowing to mankind. This is beautifully expressed in the first chapter in the constitution on the sacred liturgy[13], which goes on to declare that the renewal in the Eucharist of the covenant between the people and the lord draws the faithful and sets them ablaze with Christ's compelling love. The authors further indicate that from the Eucharist, grace is poured forth upon mankind as from a fountain. Man's sanctification in Christ and Gods glorification is achieved with maximum effectiveness. (Sacrosanctum Concillium, 1963)

We are encouraged to go and experience the real presence of grace in the Eucharist. It is a fact that if we sit with the lord in the Eucharist, gazing at him and He gazing at us, a transformation will begin to occur in our soul. Jesus requires faithfulness from us and He will accomplish the rest in our soul. This supernatural grace can be likened to the rays of the sun streaming thorough nature to bring warmth and life to creation. The sun rays assume different hues depending on the medium they cross. Likewise the supernatural graces from the throne of God are manifested differently, by different charisms (Gifts from the Holy Spirit) displayed in different individual, strengthening the individual natural talents for the good of the church. For example, the preacher will leave you enlightened and challenged to change. The hymns will seem to speak to your circumstances. A confessor will bring Gods healing love and peace. An Asher will make you feel just valued and cared for etc. Let us also consider the fact that we will not sit in the sun for long without feeling and seeing the impact of the sun's rays. We feel the warmth and sometimes the skin tones. The same way we cannot expose ourselves to the Divine graces in the sacraments without feeling the warmth and most likely our behaviors will be toned and thus a noticeable change will be obvious to others and ourselves.

God's grace working on us can be compared to a child learning to bake a cake with her mother. The mother gathers all the ingredients. Then, they mix the stuff together. The mother does most of the work and when they are done, the child will be proud that she made a cake. But in reality the mother did all the work, and provided most of the energy. Likewise in the working of Grace God does all the work and we like to take all the credit as if we did it on our own.

In the Gospels, when Jesus says that "I am the bread of life" He brings to the forefront the concept of the Eucharist. Jesus is clear that whoever comes to him will never hunger and whoever believes in him will never thirst. Jesus explicitly refers to himself in the blessed Eucharist, as the heavenly bread: "I am the living bread which comes down from heaven; if any man eats of this bread, he shall live forever" (John: 6; 35, 51).

Let's consider for a while that a person dear to you is about to die or go away for a long time in a foreign land. Probably you would share a meal with that person and in your heart of hearts, you would be sad because of the fear of the unknown; you are not sure if you will ever see that person again. After the meal, you spend the evening together watching the setting sun, or watching a brook of water in rivulet. This person then, gives you a gift as a remembrance. Most likely when you miss that person, you would go back to the same spot and the very act will bring back fond memories.

Well, Jesus plan to remain with us as the bread of life is even more powerful than that, he truly wants to be with us, providing us with the same support, love and understanding as he would do in person. But for most of the time, we can't seem to see his presence in the Eucharist for what it is? He desires to infuse us with His own life. If we become one with him, then we will share and live the life he lived. Jesus was in constant communion with his father. We can imitate him, and by eating his body, we will be in communion with the triune God; the father, Jesus and the Holy Spirit. Our souls will be united with the triune God. We will start to live our eternity with the trinity, from here below. Although humanly speaking, we may experience doubts from time to time; Jesus wants our faith and commitment. That is to totally trust in this great mystery though veiled from our human capacity to grasp its immensity and power.

Let us then approach Jesus the fountain of life and wisdom. St Alphonsus De Liguori[14] believes that this love is also referred to as a living fountain of fire and charity. He continues to say that love is the water which satisfies our thirst and that he who loves God with his whole heart neither seeks nor desires anything else. That is because in God he finds every good. Thus satisfied with God a soul is able to often exclaim "my God and my all" my God, thou art my whole good. This truly is pure blessedness and captures the essence of life. To know we are truly loved unconditionally and to love back unreservedly to one who loved us first. "O blessed soul that has found this secret that God alone suffices".

In the same book, Liguori, points out that St. Teresa[15] noted that in this world, it is impossible for all the subjects to speak to the king. St. Teresa maintains that a poor individual may actually need a third party to relay some information to the king. But to Jesus, the king of kings and lord of lords, there is no need for third parties, for everyone who wishes can find him in the Most Holy sacrament of the alter. For he says come all you; poor, rich, empty, infirm, your afflicted, you sinners, you who long to be fulfilled, and I will refresh you. Jesus is so much unlike us; we like to choose cliques of the people whom, we want to keep company with. Jesus has his hands wide open to embrace each and every one of us so long as we approach him. His heart burns with fire for our love, each one of us.

It is documented that in the Vatican council 11, on the sacred mystery of the Eucharist that our savior instituted the Eucharistic sacrifice of his body and blood to entrust to his beloved spouse, the church, a memorial of his death and resurrection: a sacrament of love, sign of unity, a bond of charity, where the mind is filled with grace and a pledge of future glory. In the Eucharist, we join our prayers with the other prayers of our brothers and sisters from all over the world. It is clear that in the Eucharistic adoration, we encounter the mystical body of Christ; the whole of humanity is joined by the rays of God love, which flows from his heart to all his children. Let's consider that Jesus is more like a parent. A sensitive Parent will give more love and support to their sick or vulnerable child than to the child, who is doing just fine. The same way God seems to care more for his weak and hurting children than those who are doing fine. Thus, the Eucharist unites all of humanity by its sacred bond of love, the lost, the weak, the marginalized and all who come to him looking for solace.

In the brief, summarizing the Catechism of the Catholic Church teaching on Blessed Eucharist, the Eucharist is considered as the heart and the summit of the church's life, for in it, Christ unites his church and all its members with his sacrifice of praise and thanksgiving offered once, and for all on the cross to his father. This sacrifice pours out the graces of salvation, on his body, the church. (1407)

The church further teaches that during consecration in the mass, the transubstantiation of the bread and wine into the body and blood of Christ is brought about. Thus Christ himself, living and glorious, is present in a true, real, and substantial manner, as laid out in the council of Trent[16], this is his body, and his blood, with his soul and his divinity. (1413).

Again, taking the body and blood of Christ increases the communicants union with the lord forgives ones venial sins and preserves him from mortal sin. This effect occurs because receiving this sacrament strengthens the unity of love between the faithful and Christ, reinforcing the bond of the church as the mystical body of Christ, (1416).

In revelations to Sr.Anna Ali[17], Jesus states that in the sacrament of his love, he represents himself completely in the form of a banquet. Jesus continues to say that in each particle of the blessed Host, he is very present just as he is at the right hand of the Eternal Father. He says that he leaves himself in this mystery in order to give souls, good and blessed chance to practice true faith, so that souls may know his mysteries so amazing. Jesus point out that it's his great love for mankind that keeps him in this form and exposed to all the humiliations. As I am exposed, Jesus says, I will pour the treasures of my infinite mercy in the human souls. It's important to note that the Lord Jesus declares that in the sacrament of his love, is a mystery which exceeds all powers. He hides his countenance so that man may have a good opportunity to practice faith. Fr Rohr[18] beautifully captures this real presence of Jesus in the Eucharist.

"In contemplation there is no argument about real presence. People who can simply be present will know about presence, union and even ecstasy, and they would not think about denying God's availability in the material world…. He continues to expound that God is calling everyone and everything home, not just picking and choosing a few…" Even as we try to expound this mystery, there is a lot we do not grasp with our finite brains, because God is so broad, than we can ever wrap around with our imagination, about His Divinity. We can only approach him with our faith and then He promised to do the rest for us.

What a consolation to know that God is seeking all of his children, and all of creation to bring them to union with himself, by means of this Eucharistic presence. As it is written in St. Paul letter to the Colossians 1; 16-20; "for in him all things were created in heaven and on earth, visible and invisible, all things were created through him and for him, and through him reconcile all things for him". As Fr.Burghardt[19] put it, the Eucharist is above all a sacrament of oneness, by making men one with Christ, and then one with one another in Christ. It would seem in the real presence of Jesus, we are healed of our internal dichotomies. It's only after we have been healed of our internal conflicts that we can in turn heal the divisions in the world. For just as we would expect a person with a toothache to take care of their pain first, so likewise in the divine presence we take care of our pains first, and then we in turn can take care of others pain as well.

What is mercy?

There are different dictionary explanations for mercy. According to the Catholic encyclopedia, Mercy is that moral virtue whereby one treats other human beings with compassion and offers spiritual/or temporal aid according to the person's wants. It is the fulfilment of the law to love one's neighbors as one's self. As well, Pope Francis has delved in depth during this year of mercy on practical ways to practice mercy as individuals, and as a church. He calls the mystery of mercy fountain of joy, serenity, and peace.[20] Again Cardinal Kasper[20], rightly declares that we must be silent about God if we don't know how to speak anew, the message of Gods mercy to the people who are in so much physical and spiritual distress.

Mercy is one of the essential attributes of God. The old and new testament is about the revelation of God of mercy, and grace to fallen human person. In the Gospel according to St. John in the prologue, it's stated clearly that "from his fullness we have all received grace in place of grace". One understanding of this passage is that grace in place of grace stands for the replacement of the old covenant by the new covenant. In the old covenant a lamb was sacrificed to seal the covenant. In the new covenant Jesus is the new Lamb of God who takes away the sins of the world. Jesus died to pay our debts; it is the greatest act of mercy to die for another so that they can be free.

In the old testament, in Deuteronomy 7:9,, the lord our God is described as the faithful God, who keeps his covenant and love constantly a thousand generations towards those who love him and keep his commandments. This covenant when summarized means to love our God with all our heart, and soul and to love our neighbor as we love ourselves.

In the Gospel according to St. Luke 6:36 we are called to be merciful as our father is merciful. This in a deeper sense is tied to Jesus teaching about love of our-selves, neighbors and enemies. Unlike the Old Testament which encouraged its followers to love their neighbor and hate their enemy, Jesus requires that His followers should love their enemies and pray for those who persecute them. Jesus points out that there is nothing special about loving ones friends, even gangs do that. What is really radical in Jesus teaching is loving and being merciful to someone who does not deserve our love. That really speaks for itself. Jesus tells his followers in order to be the children of God, they must be like God who causes rain and sun to rain and shine on the bad and good alike.

In the great psalm of King David, Psalm 51, King David invokes the great mercy of God, asking God out of His abundant compassion to blot out King David's offences. This idea of God's mercy is further developed in the New Testament where the disciples of Jesus are bound to be merciful like God our Father. For example in our Lord's Prayer, it requires us to forgive others as God forgives us. In order to be perfect as our heavenly father is perfect, we must learn to forgive absolutely without limit "and if a brother wrongs you seven times in a day and returns seven times saying 'I am sorry' you should forgive him" if you are like me by the third time, you would be thinking, do they think I am only sitting around waiting to forgive them again and again, no way. But if we call ourselves Christians, and thus profess to be Christ-like then forgiveness should have a deep meaning in our lives, as we encounter the other who needs forgiveness from us. We should also remember we need to be forgiven many times by others.

This attribute of mercy is also associated with the concept of love. Jesus repeatedly mentioned that to love the Lord our God with all our heart and to love our neighbor as we love ourselves summarize the whole of the Old Testament. Which in the Kantian categorical imperative has been termed as the golden rule ' Act on that maxim through which you can at the same time will that it should become a universal law'[22] if we like to be forgiven, loved, understood, trusted and even given a second chance, etc., so does our friend, neighbor, spouse, children and enemies too. It sounds so easy and simple in theory, but in reality it requires an extra-ordinary grace or a supernatural grace. The venerable Saint Francis of Assisi captures this attribute of mercy in a subtle way in his peace prayer.

"Make me a channel of your peace, where there is hatred, let me bring love, where injury, your pardon lord and where there's doubt, true faith in you. Make me a channel of your peace. Where there's despair in life, let me bring hope. Where there is darkness only light and where there is sadness ever joy. O master, grant that I may never seek so much to be consoled as to console, to be understood as to understand, to be loved as to love, with all my soul. Make me a channel of your peace. It is in pardoning that we are pardoned, in giving of our selves we receive and in dying that we're born to eternal life."[23]

St Francis, who through constant union with God in prayer had been transformed to be Christ-like in his love and compassion for humanity, is a perfect example of what mercy truly means.

In various rules of conduct in Leviticus 19:18, captures this idea of mercy of God by exclaiming "take no revenge and cherish no grudge against your fellow countrymen. You shall love your neighbor as yourself". In first John 3:14 this passage goes a step further to explain that we will know that we have passed from death to life if we love our brothers. In the New Testament, and particularly the epistles, stress on the importance of Christian charity on the life of Christians. The writers encourage the early Christian communities to live harmoniously as they wait for the second coming of Christ. These include intense love for one another, and hospitality without complaining. The letters encourage them to use the gifts God has given them to serve each other and to be faithful stewards of the grace of God.

In Psalm 103 which praises divine goodness, the psalmist sings of God's love and compassion which surrounds his children, God is depicted as merciful and gracious; slow to anger, abounding in kindness. The psalmist declares that as the father had compassion on his children, so does the Lord have compassion on the faithful. God is constantly reassuring us of his loving kindness through all the generations. He reminds us that nothing can come between us and his love.

Mary full of Grace

To put the work of grace in context it would be good to look at a person whom the angel described as "Full of Grace". In the gospel according to Luke 1:26-37, the Angel Gabriel during the Annunciation proclaimed to the teenage Mary mother of God, as filled with Grace. She was perfectly filled with God's favor not just a quarter, half-filled or three quarters filled. So what did that really mean? A closer look reveals that unlike the earlier prophets who would try to dissuade God that they were not able or capable or were afraid, Mary declared the fiat "I am the Hand maid of the lord, May it be done to me according to your word". She did not protest, argue, or put on a drama about her lowly state. She believed, even when troubled she only asked for clarification, "how would this happen since I do not know a man"

Holy mother Mary complied with Gods work within her, though we may point out that she was already sanctified before birth by God's sanctifying grace, and that she was naturally disposed to cooperate with God's grace already at work in her life. It appears that, the ability to trust is linked to the capacity to receive God's grace. No trust equals no capacity to receive grace, little trust results in little capacity for grace and of course great trust translates to great capacity to obtain God's favor.

Divine mercy

Although Gods mercy is the central message of the whole Bible, St. Faustina Kowalski is designated as the apostle of Divine mercy. In February 22, 1931, she saw a vision of Jesus with rays of mercy streaming from His heart. Jesus charged her to start recording a journal so that others would come to know and trust in Jesus. In the diary of Faustina, the lord on several occasions reveals that his heart is on fire desiring to outpour its love to humankind, but Jesus is more than a gentleman, he will not impose his wish on us. Water flowed from the side of Jesus indicating his great mercy for the world. In the Gospel according to John 19:34 God declares that. "I sent prophets wielding thunderbolts to my people. Today I am sending you with my mercy to the people of the whole world. I do not want to punish aching mankind, but I desire to heal it, pressing it to My Merciful Heart." (*Diary*, 1588)[24] Jesus is the Divine physician, he knows that we his children are sick and hurting. He longs to embrace us in his healing love, if we let him. What is holding us back then?

It is recounted in the book of Edith Stain[25], in the works of St. Teresa that, St. Teresa of Jesus was transported to hell in a vision just for a moment. St. Teresa mentioned that she recognized what God's goodness had preserved her from. She actually believed that the superscription for her life should read "the mercy of God"[26] since she could not extol God's mercy throughout the world, she at least wanted to gather some selected souls around her who would commit themselves to withdrawal, constant prayer, poverty and a strict life style of prayer.

Now what?

During the New Year's 2016 speech[27], Pope Francis issued a caution that "the enemy of peace isn't only war, but also indifference," and he denounced "barriers, suspicions, fears and closures" toward others. Pope Francis further challenged us to reflect on some disturbing facts like "Sometimes we ask ourselves how it is possible that human injustice persists unabated and that the arrogance of the powerful continues to demean the weak, relegating them to the most squalid outskirts of our world." He continued: "We ask how long human evil will continue to sow violence and hatred in our world, reaping innocent victims." These are serious challenges which leave us hoping for more answers.

Although this is a very complex matter, if we are merciful we would treat others as we would like to be treated, no one wants to be put down, mistreated or demeaned in any form. But for some reason this is hard for most of us to grasp, we never really get it. We are selfish and egocentric, we like the world to revolve around us and meet our needs at any cost. But the truth is we are all connected. Unless we become aware that one person's hurting because of our indifference or inaction is like letting our pinky toe rot because we think somehow it's insignificant and dispensable.

It's not until our whole leg gets gangrenous and has to be cut off or our whole body becomes septic and we have to die due to our neglect that we realize how important each part is. We should not neglect any part of humanity if it's in our power to do something about it, otherwise the whole body may get septic and die as a result. Again these barriers, suspicions, fears and judgmental attitudes may be one of the many reasons people are disillusioned by the church experience. The Christian Science monitor[28] had detailed first hand experiences why some people were frustrated by what they referred to as "Sunday morning experience" Many are uneasy with the judgmental interpretation of the church teachings. Many are also uneasy with how this exclusivity translates into treatment of those outside the fold.

The church is a powerful expression of God's presence but the churches teaching interpretations need to be seen through the eyes of a merciful God and father not a self-serving distant tyrant. In Mathew Kelly's[29] book rediscover Christ, Kelly talks of miracles that abound all the time. Kelly talks about a friend who found a way to bring God's mercy every time he went to a social setting. The said friend would always look for someone suffering, most likely feeling out of place and he would spent time with that person. This is something we can all take for granted until we go out of our familiar settings and become the outsider. This brings us to the realization that we can practice God mercy and love, most of the time if we are attentive to the inner promptings of the spirit of God.

During this year of mercy, the church is calling us to re-experience Gods loving kindness to each one of us. God cares for each one of us as if each of us was the only person God was trying to reach out to. God says even if a mother should forsake her child, He will not abandon his own. God is so much in love with us that he holds us in the palm of his hands. He continues to allude that even if the earth should quake, the mountain shake, and the ocean roar, his power would protect us. Throughout the Bible God uses different imagery to show us how much he cares and loves us, all through life. He is a rock of refuge, a fortress, a shield and a sure defense. We do not earn this by our own ability, it's God's pure gift to us if we turn and trust him. Just Like a child trusts its mother for care, so does God expects us to trust in his love and mercy.

On Good Friday his heart was pierced with a lance, and blood and water gushed from his side. Jesus became the pascal sacrifice, the unblemished lamb, offered for our sanctification; Just as the Israelites were saved by the blood of the lamb which was sprinkled to the lintel and the door post, when the Angel passed over the house of the Israelites, but dealt death to the first born sons of Egyptians. By this the children of Israel were released from Egypt, and allowed to start their journey to the Promised Land. Likewise by the blood of Jesus we were freed from slavery of sin, redeeming us to be children of God. We truly are the adopted children of God, heir's princesses and princes of the kingdom.

We, like King David in Psalm 51, need just to be aware of our need for God's mercy and compassion.

David reminds God to have mercy on him out of God's goodness. If we can see our state for what it is, a state of human weakness, and acknowledge that God is all good and desires our wellbeing more than we desire it for ourselves, then we would run to him like a child ready to be embraced in God's loving hands.

"In your abundant compassion blot out my offense". David is aware that God is rich in kindness and able to wipe away his sins. Most often we do not know how to forgive others or even ourselves completely and thus we confuse Gods ability to forgive us, with our inability to forgive ourselves or others. The truth is that God does forgive us completely. The fact is that even though God forgives completely the effects or the consequences of sin may remain forever. For example, in David's case, Uriah the Hittite was dead, and his wife Beersheba bore a son, with King David.

"In my inmost being teach me wisdom", and as we know the fear of the Lord is the beginning of wisdom. It's one thing to act holy or wise but the marker of holiness is the things we choose to do, when no one else can see or give us credit for doing them. This may be one interpretation for what King David was longing for. He had ordered Uriah to be placed where the battle was heavy so that he could be killed and still king David maintained a perfect cover- up. But God, who sees all, send a prophet to King David. We can only conclude that King David was faced with the reality that although he did look innocent humanly speaking, God saw his hidden thoughts and deeds. Only God can Grant the grace of Divine Knowledge in the soul of his people. This draws us back to the psalms which keep pointing to the necessity of meditating on the word of the lord often (day and night), so that we can be like the tree planted beside the running waters whereby the leaves are ever green.

"Renew in me a steadfast spirit" This is really King David praying for an unwavering dedication to God. It's important to note that Grace is a free gift of God, we cannot earn it by our merit, but we can pray to God to grant us the favor of renewed zeal and vigor in doing his will. To paraphrase this, we can earn renewed dedication in spirit by praying and yearning for it. God does say he will take the heart of stone away and give his people a new heart and put his new spirit in them (Ezekiel 11;19) so that his people may observe his statutes, and carry out his decrees. Sometimes it does look like we are in the mercy of our whims, but if we borrow a leaf from this psalm maybe, what we need is to remain focused long enough in search of God, then God will bless us with this spirit of fortitude.

Finally the psalmist does beg God not to cut him off "Do not drive me from your presence, nor take from me your Holy Spirit" This is a sincere longing for King David not to be cast away from God's service. We see similar prayer by king Solomon the son of David when he prays for wisdom admitting that he is human, weak and short-lived, lacking in understanding, judgement and laws.(Wisdom 9: 4-5). Were these two kings great because they prayed and longed for wisdom? Or were they wise kings who became great. A close look at both kings reveals that David was a repentant sinner who prayed for God's Grace or wisdom to help him. As well the study of the Bible reveals that King Solomon was a weak man who prayed for Gods wisdom and everything else fell in place.

In this year of mercy we can look up to these great men of God and take courage in knowing they put their trust in God's great love and compassion for humankind and they were not put to shame.

Allegory of Clear glass

Our life is like a house made of glass wall. The Grace of God is like the sun rays. If due to sloth or whatever other reason we let the wall glass get dirt, the sun rays will not illuminate the house. The dirt in the glass will become a barrier and prevent the sun rays from being reflected into the interior of the house. On the other hand if we clean the glass, the sun rays will radiate through and illuminate the whole house. Likewise in our Christian living, we should take care and clean our glass, that is, become aware of whom we are, by being the best of who we were meant to be. After cleaning the glass of our lives, God's grace will shine through us unrestrained and the effects of Grace will be obvious in our lives and the lives of others. So let's get our ego, selfishness and pride out of our way, by going to confessions, fasting, prayer and alms giving.

Another effect when you illuminate the house with the sun rays is that you will have a clear view on the state of the interior setting. Any small crack will become visible. It is not that the house has become cracked after the illumination.

No, it's because now there is enough light to have a clear vision and see any faults which were oblivious when the house was not well illuminated. The same can be compared to our interior life when we start to live a life of grace; suddenly we start to see many little cracks which were oblivious initially when Christ was not the center of our being.

What happens when we enter a room which is dark? We stagger in the darkness, bump into objects and sometimes we imagine there are monsters because we make them out of our minds. This is also true when we are living undisplined lives. We stumble in the dark, can't make out objects clearly. We mistake a rope for a snake. It's uncomfortable to work in darkness, we take forever to finish activities, but once we have the light, we see all things clearly. We can easily differentiate a rope from a snake. The same principle can be applied to our spiritual lives when we are not living in the values of the gospel we are living in the dark, we can easily confuse what is right and what is morally wrong. It is a hit and miss game of living. But once we are living on Grace or the Gospel values, things fall in place and we can see clearly. We become a light in the darkness for ourselves and for others. Let's not get discouraged when we fail, let's wake up and continue with our journey to our promised land. May grace, mercy and love follow you all the days of our life.

Index

References

1. Accademia (ND) Michelangelo's prisoner's circa 1520-23, (Accademia gallery in Florence) retrieved from http://www.accademia.org/ explore- museum/artworks/Michelangelo's-prisoners-slaves

2. Wikipedia, the free. Encyclopedia retrieved from en.wikipedia.org/ wiki/Fountain of Life.

3. M.G. Easton M.A., D.D., Illustrated Bible Dictionary, Third Edition, published by Thomas Nelson, 1897.

4. Broderick, R. C. (1976). *The Catholic Encyclopedia*. T. Nelson.

5. Pope Francis (2015) the holy year of mercy: A faith-sharing quide with reflection by Pope Francis.

6. *Writings (1958): [The Fount of Knowledge]*. Fathers of the Church, inc.: Vol. 37.

7. O'Connor, J.B. (1910). St. John Damascene. In The Catholic Encyclopedia. New York: Robert Appleton Company. Retrieved January 3d, 2016 from New Advent: http://www.newadvent.org/ cathen/08459b.htm

8. Ryan, J. K., Pilkington, J. G., & Pusey, E. B. (1960). *The Confessions of St. Augustine*. International Collector's Library.

9. Foley J. (1978) text and music.

10. Merriam Webster online dictionary retrieved August 29, 2015, from http://www.merriam-webster.com/dictionary/grace

11. Flannery, A. (Ed.). (1996). *Vatican Council II: Constitutions, Decrees, and Declarations: The Basic Sixteen Documents*. North port, NY: Costello Pub.co.

12. Flynn, Vinny (2015) 7 Secrets of Divine Mercy. DeKalb, Illinois: Ignatius Press- Lighthouse Catholic Media.

13. Pohle, J. (1909). Actual Grace. In The Catholic Encyclopedia. New York: Robert Appleton Company. Retrieved January 7, 2016 from New Advent: http://www.newadvent.org/cathen/06689x.htm

14. See, H. (1994). *Catechism of the Catholic Church*. Citta del Vaticano: Libreria Editrice vaticana.

15. Liguori, S. A., & De' Liguori, A. M. (1994). Holy Eucharist. St. Teresa of Avila (1989) (Allison, p. Trans.) Interior Castle. New York: An Image book.

16. Schroeder, H. J. (1941). *Canons and Decrees of the Council of Trent*. London: B. Herder book Company

17. Sr.Anna Ali (1994), On the Eucharist: A Divine Appeal. Clifton, VA: Met enterprises ltd.

18. Rohr, R. (2008). Things Hidden: Scripture as Spirituality. Cincinnati, OH: St. Anthony Messenger press.

19. Burghardt, W., (1961) Sermons on Theology and life: All Lost in Wonder. Westminster, Maryland: The Newman Press.

20. Pope Francis (2014) the church of mercy: A vision for the church. Illinois, Chicago: Loyola Press

21. Kasper (2014) MERCY; The essence of the Gospel and the key to Christion life (M. William, Trans). Mahwah, NJ: Paulist press. (Original work polished 2012)

22. Grosch, P., Large, W., Wenham, D., Appleton, J., Astley, J., Fiddes, P., & Hick, J. Kant's Categorical Imperative

23. Robinson, M. (1999). *St. Francis of Assisi: the legend and the life*. A&C Black.

24. Kowalski, F. (1987). Divine Mercy in My Soul. The Diary of Sister M. Faustina.

25. Stein, S. E. (1992), Gelber, L., & Linssen, M. (Eds.) *The Hidden Life: Hagiographic Essays, Meditations, Spiritual Texts* (Vol. 4). Washington, DC: Ics Publications.

26. Saint Teresa (of Avila). (1980*). the collected works of St. Teresa of Avila.* Institute of Carmelite Studies.

27. D'EMILIO, F. (2016, Jan, 1st) Pope: now's the time to end indifference "false neutrality" Associated press retrieved from http://news.yahoo.com/pope-nows-time-end-indifference-false- neutrality-100858348.html

28. Bruinius, H. (2015, Dec, 19th) why these Americans are "Done" with church, but not God. (The Christian Science Monitor) retrieved from http://www.csmonitor.com/USA/Society/2015/1219/Why-these- Americans-are-done-with-church-but-not-with-God

29. Kelly, M. (2015) Rediscovering Jesus, An invitation USA: Beacon Publishing.